POETRY
Within
THE STATE

Emmett Corbett

978-1-917728-27-0 Second Edition © 2025 Emmett Corbett
978-1-915502-84-1 First edition
All rights reserved. No part of this book may be reproduced, stored in a retrieval system, or transmitted by any means, electronic, mechanical, photocopying, recording or otherwise without written permission from the author. Published in Ireland by Orla Kelly Publishing. Artwork copyright Emmett Corbett.

Orla Kelly Publishing
27 Kilbrody,
Mount Oval,
Rochestown,
Cork,
Ireland.

Preface

'Poetry within the State' invites readers to traverse a landscape wrought with the stark realities of modern Ireland, vividly conveyed through a collection of poems. This collection shares potent insights of social critique, entwining strands of hypocrisy and double standards with threads of injustice stitching through the fabric of today's society.

The poet's voice oscillates between anger and advocacy, despair and devotion, capturing the depths of societal two-tier systems and the enduring human struggle to live by one's moral compass.

The poems in "Poetry within the State" are not mere words arranged upon a page; they are a pulsating heartbeat of awareness, an outcry for change that echoes the silent murmurs of the unnoticed in Irish society. They serve as a profound exploration of confronting social problems—inequality, human rights issues, and the dynamic face of injustice.

Yet, amidst the critical observation lies a core of spirituality. Some verses are whispered prayers, seeking solace and guidance in a higher power, offering gratitude and seeking divine direction amidst the chaos of worldly challenges.

For every reader who has witnessed or been scarred by disparity, 'Poetry within the State' offers not just words on injustice, but also an invitation to feel, reflect, and perhaps join in advocating for a more equitable future.

Indulge in this deep, heartfelt collection to experience a powerful blend of social commentary and poetic grace.

They say you can't judge a book by its cover, but you can get a fairly good idea of what genre it is.

Contents

Blackbird	1
Republic	2
Rhetoric	4
Locked Out	7
The Lie	8
Society	9
Same Old Thing	10
Hypocrites	13
Alcoholic	16
Domestic	18
Melancholy	19
Life	20
Celtic Queen	22
Sugar Daddy	23
Bachelors Haste	24
Spinster's Haste	26
Procrastinate	27
Sleep	28
Bouncer	29
Junkie	32
True Grit	34
Gen Z	35
What's Going on	38
Truth	41
Androgynous	43

Exchequer	44
Justice	45
Fields	46
Ivory Tower	47
Mommy	48
Undercurrent	49
Praise YAH	50
Promise	52
Judgment	53
Regret	54
My God	55
Salvation	56
Patience	57
Grace	58
Torch of Fidelity	59
Please Review	61
About the Author	62

Blackbird

Paddy in the doorway
Paddy in the field
Paddy cold and broken
As the blackbird flaps its wings.
Paddy is excluded
Paddy is dismissed
Paddy is precluded
As the blackbird fluffs its nest.
Paddy struggles hopeless
Forage day to day
Daunted by his circumstance
While the blackbirds prance and play.
Paddy dares not provoke, duplicity perceived
For he dreads the angry squawking flocks,
of blackbird caws and shrieks.
The blackbirds prosper easy, as they flourish with their chicks
While Paddy has no home abode
To live life with his kids.
Paddy's bread is eaten
Forgotten oh so soon
For the vain labours of Paddy, are the efforts of a fool.
Paddy in the doorway
Paddy in the field
Destitute and wanting
As the blackbirds dance and sing.

Republic

This is your Republic
Thank you for your loss
Thank you for your sweat and tears
Your fathers blood it cost.

This is your Republic
Now let us run the show
Our posterity will rule you right
Controlled forever more.

This is your Republic
We do now what we please
Frail cowards hound the ancient gaels
Dispatched across the seas.

This is your Republic
We won't evict you off the land
But you can't buy and you can't rent
For this state is built on sand.

This is your Republic
Your sacrifice was cheap
Sold-out to the vulture funds
And bought up by the east.

This is your Republic
Who dares to take us on?
For we pay oafs, who know no oaths
And never see no wrong.

This is your Republic
Transparency of lies
Your sons who dare expose our deeds
We teach you to despise.

This is your Republic
No bananas over here
But we've got Tech and Pharma-chem
And tax breaks for our peers.

This is your democracy
Now sit down and shut your mouth
Your opinion that of simpletons
Your protests are for louts.

This is our Republic
One hundred years delayed
For we removed your Holy God
And stand here in His place.

Rhetoric

Where is their international covenant?
Where is their international bill?
Where are their lauded landmark documents?
Where's their framework
While they kill?

Where's their comprehensive values?
Where is their universal declaration?
Where's their indivisible core principles?
Champions of rights alleged inalienable?

Where are their thought-out treaties?
Where are their chartered fundamentals?
Where are their binding rules of governance
That they promote so instrumental?

Where are their obligations?
Where are their constitutions?
Where's their conventions on protection
Outside their noble institutions?

Where is your wise old council?
Oh, honourable humanitarian.
What use is peace promoted
When enforcement on vacation?

Where are their neighbourly relations?
Where is their transnational peace?
Cooperation given cautiously
Prevent the threats to cease.

Where's self-determination
Endorsing human rights?
As fundamental freedoms preached so pious
Evaporate from sight

Within their fickle forum
They harmonize their deeds
Their frivolous diplomacy
Paves paths for global greed.

Where are their underlying tenets?
Where are their statutes for sovereign dignity?
No hiding for the hungry
Is their sanctioned pledged complicity

Where's their public services?
And cohesive cause for charity
Their absent interference
Upholds their present-day disparity.

Where is their free movement,
Migrating through their streets?
Past their flimsy national borders
With floods of refugees.

Where is their sustainable development?
And environmental laws?
Where is their abhorrence of emissions?
For land poisoned with bombs.

Where is their social justice?
And their tolerant respect
While they lecture integration
To all outside their sect.

Where is their condemnation?
At apartheid form their creed
And despised discrimination
While the babes and mothers bleed.

Can paper shield from bullets?
Can hot air blow shells off course?
Can speeches stall starvation?
Can the defenceless fight with force?

Where is their benevolent inclusion?
Where's their diversity?
In the west they call it fascism
But in the east its unity.

Locked Out

Beyond our box room windows
The construction tiger moans
Homes are built vainglorious
But who can get the loan?
Listen to the soundbites
"Engineering tides to raise all boats"
Platitudes of rhetoric
Yet nowhere to hang our coats.
Within our family's front rooms, sipping cups of tea
Watch the dream homes be erected, upon our old TVs
This housing ladder slimy
So can find their feet
Precisely polished at the first rung
Greased with gluttony and greed
The vacant path to housing, reveals dead-ends at no small cost
Boarded up and blocked off
The symbolism is not lost.

The Lie

First begins frustration
Followed by offence
Then begins resentment
Though no harm was ever meant.

Then ensues the envy
For no unrighteous fault
Shadowed by raw jealously
Sewn deep within the heart.

On pursuit of sad vindictiveness
Now conceives the lie
Forming baseless slanders
Wishing your demise.

The unfounded slurs soon spread
Whispered ear to ear
Maturing into gossip
For everyone to hear.

The hearsay then is echoed
Though its few who know the facts
Fictious falsehoods flourish
To compensate for what they lack.

Twisted tales grow exponential
Just to kick you when you're low
As you rise with real integrity
Refuting all the spite they've sown.

Society

Imitate!
But how can I conform today?
Should I submit to your dogmatic way?
And everything that you say.
Pursue
All that you do
Comply
And hope you approve.
Is it better for me?
When you're speaking for me
While existing, being told that I'm free.
Should I grant my acceptance?
Vainly
In hope of acceptance
Or be alone, unconcerned with rejection.
Here are some questions, to life's intersection
Who but God can give righteous direction?

Same Old Thing

It's the same old thing
But a different day
The same old ding dong
I hear you say.
The same old pubs
The same old clubs
The same old buzz, from the same old drugs.
The same old faces
In the same old places
The same old bookies
with the same old races.
The same old dole
Squandered on the same old waste
Eating the same old food, with the same old taste.
The same old news, at the same old time
Discussing the same old politics
Exposed of the same old crime
With the same new politicians
That went to the same old schools
Telling the same old lies, to the same old fools.
To the same old public
with the same old complaints
Looking for the same old promises
and the same old change.
Believing the same old threats, with the same old fear
Lost in the same old distractions
with the same old cares.

It's just the same old pantomime, using the same old puppets
Providing the same fake hope
in the same false prophets
Disregarding your same old opinion, with the same deaf ears
Then you die from the same old disease
in the same young years.
For it's the same old scape-goat, that gets the same old blame
From the same old Devil, in this age-old game.

They say the pen is mightier than the sword.
Only because, it is the pen, that has the protentional
to capture the hearts and minds of men,
inspiring courage, self-sacrifice, and perseverance.
Thus, mobilising the sword.

Hypocrites

English tyrant, Irish tyrant
Tis all the same to me
Behold the Irish patriot upon his comfy seat
Behold the new regime, but alas, there is nothing new
Exchanging black and tan, for different shades of blue.
As boys, they told the teacher, now as men they tell the judge
Vindictive lies of vengeance fulfil their petty grudge
Don't question their authority, or dare resist control
For the boot is on the other foot, to kick you down the hole.
Do you have a problem with Guards? says he, with the permanent expression of contempt etched into his face
Nah, not me, I've got no problem with Guards
My problem's with double standards and abuse, authority being misused
Injustice and corruption, people's lives and their destruction.
I got a problem with unprofessional disrespect, code of conduct and its neglect
I got a problem with looking down your nose, and laughing up your sleeves
I got a problem with policing blue-collar people, for white-collar thieves.
I got a problem with cronyism, nepotism, gangsterism, traitorous' protectionism of government crooks, and slap-on-the-wrist-ism
I got a problem with perjurious fabrication and omission of facts.

I got a problem with squandering funds and resources acquired through tax
For real, no more tribunals we need, just put the money into housing
cause we need somewhere to sleep.
I got a problem with soft boys, being abusive, thinking their tough
and the tough boys standing by, keeping their mouth shut.
I got a problem with being handcuffed, for peacefully not engaging when asked for my name
Then being told I got the right to remain silent, when been taken away!
I got a problem with having different laws for different people, impartiality being feeble
and judicious apes that see, speak and hear no evil
I got a problem with the judiciaries 20/20 vision
for the rich man a fine, for the poor man the prison.
I got a problem with the words Irish and justice, being mutually exclusive
with the existence of one, rendering the other elusive
I've got a problem with oxymoron's, form poxy morons, being forced on me
I got a problem with this democracy's, dogmatic mockery.
I got a problem with Garda informants allowed to pedal poison with impunity
Causing addiction, family crisis, and death in our community!

Is information really that valuable?
I got a problem with arrogant detectives,
dismissively not detecting
or harassing real criminals, like they're water protesting
Oh, guardian please, declare what you're guarding to me
Is it I from the justice, or the justice from me?

Alcoholic

If you were anybody else
People would say you were cruel
The way I always take you out
But make me look like a fool.
Still, we got a bond
That they'll never understand
The way I'm always by your side
With you embraced in my hand.
For I can always pick you up
Every time I feel down
You help me forget about my troubles
Anytime the're around.
I empathise with other men, that be flirting with you
For your blonde and gold complexion
Has a radiant hue
They crave you on their lips
Just to savour your kiss
While pausing on a breath
Contemplating the next
So luscious
You aptly complement cigarettes
Nursing to my stress
Via rest.
Yet, money means nothing
When it comes to spending on you
Because I could never be me
If I never had you.

Yet people still talk
Saying your soaking my wealth
And even worse
Saying your affecting my health
Claiming you are to blame, every time I'm arrested
But I deny your involvement
To the judge, and contested
The courts say I should leave you
That you're the cause of my blues
But I don't care what they say
Because I'm in love with you, Boooze.

Domestic

Democracy is easily pissed
Justice quick with its fists
Me, I'm quick to duck, when they swing and they miss.
Quick to cover my head
Quick to block with my wrists
Sip your Kool-Aid, if you can't picture this.
So, picture this
Cornered by the State, bullied and shook
Tensed up, face wincing, brace for the hook.
I flee their rhetoric, like a deer from a trap
But every time I think I'm through, all I catch is the flash
Bang! there you go, back on the floor
And I won't retaliate, I'm only asking for more.
For sure.
Why?
Grey skies and black eyes
Enduring gloomy days
In a trancelike haze
I long to contemplate
A news that's not fake
Just a day without bickering
A lie without sniggering
An insult without mention
A Homeland without tension
All I really want to do is just breathe
Let me escape, for one moment
And fantasise to be free
Where I never have to dream liberty.

Melancholy

As I gaze at my reflection
Many miles from vanity
Discouraged
I might catch a glimpse of insanity.
I pause upon the world and ponder
Deep past my retina
Sharp visions, rip my focus asunder
I don't want to live
I only want to see tomorrow
Sleep through the ordeal
Escape the sorrow.
Let this torment lay dormant
Yet I lay awake
Like time, I stand still
But refuse to wait.
Nonchalantly
I await my fate
Contemplate my current state
There's no joy
No hate.
Am I'm depressed?
If so, then I couldn't care less.

Life

This is Life
This is Fear
This is Self-Consciousness
This is Hate
This is Rage
This is Embarrassment
This is Humiliation
This is Rejection
This is Regret
This is Pain, this is Pain, this is Pain
This is Loneliness
This is Want
This is Desire
This is Envy
This is Jealousy
This is Bitterness
This is feeling sorry for ourselves
This is Pathetic
These are Obstacles
These are Challenges
This is Life
This is Learning
This is Experience
This is Knowledge
This is Wisdom
This is Motivation
This is Determination
This is Overcoming

Yes, this is Life
This is Real
This is Failure
This is Success
This is Weakness
This is Strength
These are Feelings
These are Emotions
This is Acknowledging
This is Understanding
This is Appreciating
This is Poetry
This is Absorbing
That-this-is-Life
And within dwells it's conquer, within dwells love.

Celtic Queen

Everything was grey, until I saw her face
And when I did, then I saw God's grace
A fair cloud and blue sky
Un-entwined in each eye
Surely nature is jealous of you
Hair gold like the sun
Skin rose like the bud
Smile soft, like the pale of the moon
Legs long to her bum, like peaches and plums
Yet smooth as a riverbed stone
Like the sunrays in May, on a spring summers day
There's splendour wherever she roams.
As a lavender field
Trailing scent on the breeze
So refreshing, so fragrant and sweet
When I beheld with my eyes, within I did sigh
For a creature so pleasant and meek
Yet I felt so alive, when monotony died
Exchanging dullness, for brightness and warmth
So unassuming
Of her beauty in blooming
Unaware to the stares that she vaunts
Then I acknowledge the Lord
For this queen that He formed
For His blessings so generous and true
For all of my days
Will I always give praise
For the day, that I laid eyes on you.

Sugar Daddy

That can't be his girlfriend
It must be his daughter
Is he buying her vodka?
Or is he buying her water?
Is it a wink of affection?
Or a wink of seduction?
Is it a date of consent?
Or a case of abduction?
The fool and his status
objects to possess
The more devious his charm
The more investment he gets
The more substance he has
The more gifts that he buys
To make up for the arrogance, delusions and the lies
The want of celebrity, dreams of a star
Who finance their fondness, along with their car
The fools and their status, objects to obtain
Pay intangible cost, for tangible gain.

Bachelors Haste

The clock is ticking
I'm not getting any younger
Don't tell me all the good ladies are gone!
For I spent my best years
In laughter and tears
Whiskey, wild women and song
That thing I desired, is now that thing I decline
While that thing that I shunned, I now yearn to be mine
Ignorant fool, such as I, yes indeed
Back then I was sure, but know today, I was green.

It's better to have perspective in the audience critiquing the mood, than to be the star of the show with lone perception.

Spinster's Haste

My biology is ticking
I'm not getting any younger
Don't tell me I can't find one hundred percent
For I don't waste my time
With eights or just nines
I have to have ten out of ten.
My haughty rejections, to strive for perfection
Swipe left, at nine and a half
He must have a salary, he must have a house
I'm not pushed about having the laugh
But while I hunt for elevens
I see sixes and sevens
Now happily married, with kids
I want what they have
But with muscles and cash
Ticking boxes, ensures excellence
But with the passing of time
I'm no longer so fine
And fail to turn heads, with the guys
Now I'm alone, swiping right on my phone
But who wants to be with a five?

Procrastinate

I'm still searching
Can anyone console this need?
I trust there is
But, where is she?
I'm still empty
Can anybody fill this void?
And if so
Then who is she?
Unfulfilled
I still wait
With desire for her
Loyal to my soul mate, I've not met
Still waiting
Still craving
For my thirst to be quenched
Soon I'll be left on the shelf
Still yearning
Still burning
Still longing for her
Until, nostalgia slowly twists to regret.

Sleep

As I slip off to the dream world
A blissful slumber,
There are things that I vaguely remember.
Visions so distant, but clear
So familiar
Leave me be!
I feel comfortable here.
I elope with the sister of death
Sleep my only relief
To my disappointment, I awake and she's left
My solitude has nothing to say
Nothing to enjoy
While facing the day
I yearn for the deep sleep
Who will never forsake me
Soon as I fall
And surrender
I know she catch me and take me.

Bouncer

Look at me, now who are you?
I've been enduring all week
but where were you?
I have my ups and downs, I'm sure you do too
Is this not life, however sad, but true
Do I not laugh, do I not cry like you?
Do I not breathe, or even bleed like you?
Am I not a man, who exists like you?
But unlike me, I don't steal from you
Steal…I observe you ponder
What do you steal?
Here, try on these shoes, in which you put so much esteem in,
and I let you know how I feel.
I don't rob a man of enjoyment, and a good night out
I don't ask him questions with suspicion,
Then listen with doubt
I don't snatch away the simple expectations, of unwinding with friends
While taking immature girls age at face value, when you know they pretend.
I don't look down my nose upon others, and act the big man
Think I'm rough, think I'm tough
With a façade that's a sham
You don't know me from Adam, you never seen me before
So why so judgemental, as I step to the door?
Can you not let me in, is this too much to ask?
But if I'm sober and steady, maybe you see a task
Maybe you see a threat

See a chore, insecure?
And realize you're not all that, without your job on the door
Is this not fact that I speak, and truth I impute?
Quick, call your gang, for a man
Just one man that disputes.
I'm still here; I'm not running,
I'm not petitioning pleas
For I rather get beat on my feet, than retreat on my knees
So, what can I call this, for dire need of a word?
Is it prejudice or intolerance, or just simply absurd?
For I can only know who I be, and only be who I am
Yet you only see the shirt and the shoes,
But never the man
Never the nature, the character or dependable friend
Never my money, the same colour, that's not worthy to spend.
And this is nothing you've learned
Just only something you're taught
How you can only put faith, in leather and cloth
While nationalities galore, are enjoying my city
Where I'm born breed and buttered
And refused, it's a pity
It's a shame; it's a disgrace this hypocrisy mockery
You have no answers to questions
You have no reasons for stopping me
But these are your actions, so let you do what you do
Because they don't reflect bad against me,
they just deflect mad towards you.
Enjoy your little ride for a while

Your little trip while it lasts
For power is always seeking new commuters, until the journey has passed
And as it draws near to your stop, and your way past your clock
Then that's when your ego will suddenly drop
Smashing in to chards, of fabrications and yarns
Your pseudo supremacy, which displayed no substance no chemistry
Is now exposed for the charade that it is.
Oh, how you can live
Now knowing that's it's a lie that you live
I sincerely pray I'll never know the answer.
Feeding off actuality, as if reality had cancer
Consuming your subjective truth
Oh, what can you do?
And what will you do?
Now that I just formed a narrow opinion
Of you?

Junkie

Young fella with addiction
Feeds his affliction
Down to the doctor, scam a prescription
Young fella got issues, so appears like a menace
Hanging around with his boys, making noise at the chemist
A couple of valium the colour of shy-blue
An if lucky a few sleepers, to give him a nice snooze
Dropping these tablets, he's a slave to his habit
Kill the pain in his brain, just to stop it from rambling
Drug dealers got coca, but most of its soda
And badly mixed heroin, to slip in a coma
Politics won't stop it, yet claim that they're on it
But young men that's alert, is the last thing they wanted
It's the last thing they need, while feeding their greed
Young fellas are distracted, engrossed without heed
Chasing a cure, that's no longer a high
Just a momentary fix, with no time to ask why
All the while they eek by, with only room to assume
That they alone are the junkies
But of course, that's not true.
Young couple with a bank loan
For a house that they don't own
Back to the banker, to give him some more dough
Young couple got debts, but scrape by under pressure
Increasing rates, payments late, money-changers going get ya
Appealing for welfare, is just a temporary repair

Slaves to a system, governing by fear
Unashamedly endorsed, with no show remorse
For politicians are tacticians at distorting the law
No homes for their people, legacies of neglect
While the banksters are the dealers, pushing interest
Perish the thought, of you ever living care free
With no debt, with no stress, just your thoughts to think free
With your views to direct, those you elect
To represent with consent, your concerns with effect
You see, the banker is the dealer
And the debt is the hit
The borrower is the junkie
And the cash is the fix
With no job to get paid, a week's wage to spend fast
To appease this disease
With injections of cash
The arrears are cold turkey, as your credit's descending
To ravenous demands which exploits your dependence
Immoral withdrawers, which exist without rule
That provides for the junkie, and robs from the fools.

True Grit

I bite off my nose
Just to spite my face
So metaphorically
I'm in an ugly place
Integrity's repulsive
But never compromise
Cause when we do
We only compensate the lies.
Never relax on the facts
Or spoof with the truths
Never tippytoe the eggshells
Never be aloof or mute
Stick to your guns on every occasion
Be quick
To slay weasel worded evasions.
The emperor naked
Unclothed and shamed
Never admire or hire
Never blame for gain
On the road less travelled
It demands true grit
To march strong
Pushing back the hypocrites.

Gen Z

Be a little bit deeper than your average fool
And don't ask the questions, that the average do
Understand what you do
Why you do,
When you do
And when it's truly your choice to choose.
Fix your gaze upon truth
As mirrors eternal, unchanged
But in this world of deceit
Which began with a lie
The truth is evermore strange.
Awake from your slumber
Realise you're more, than a number
Reclaim life that's been sold-out for bribes
Don't just survive
Be alive
Respond and do seek
Appreciate, that you're someone unique
Someone exclusive, distinctive, one of a kind
Animate every fraction of mind.
For lies are seductive
Designed as bars for our prison
From the powers that be
That prepares our decisions
They map out our routes
And directs all our paths
Where each road always leads
And ends in their traps.

Peddlers of transitory tangibles
Fit for soulless animals
Promoting vain aspirations for good looks
Downgrade our lives
Update our Facebooks.
In our minds is were losing this battle
We are more than mere cattle
Unrelenting, were choked in this grapple.
Descendants of tribes once so valiant
Abhor social dalliance.
Overcoming is legacy grasped
Such independence is real
Such promises true
Such blessings the corporate do lack.

Accountability for the negligent is justice for the neglected.

What's Going on

What's going on? I heard theses word sang in a song
But do we really ever consider the question?
Consider inspecting
Examine why there's sorrow and famine
Contemplate how there's conflict and hate
Not in shallow debates
Or superficial disapproval, passing the blame
What's going on? Who can explain?
Could it be that we're blinded, by a veil of vices and lies
And look upon these queries, and theories through bloodshot eyes?
Unaware to what's coming next
Drunk on the lusts of our flesh
The degeneration of culture, as were duped into this con
Now ask yourself, what's going on?
Why the youth are not young
Addicted, disrespectful and strung
By means of media, bad example and drugs
Not knowing self-worth, confused performing self-hurt
Abandoned by those who decide
Off the learning curve, in a whirling swerve, downward they slide
Head first to destruction, they dive.
With chips on their shoulders, decay in the attitudes
Closed down, locked up, constricted for latitude
Government don't care about you
You can protest all day, all year, they don't give a crap about you.

They're not leaders, their sell-outs and minions
Bent over, no closure
Constipated to needs and opinions
That's why when you look deep within them, they stink
Decisions made with backhanders, and winks
Right across the board, at every end of the spectrum
Politicians and judges, can't police my respecting
They can't force my allegiance
Can't win my heart, nor my mind
For they rob the wool off our backs, to pull over our eyes
Then lead us blind to the slaughter, as naked lost sheep
They are wolves in amongst us, and where the prey they do seek
Am delving too deep, I don't think that I am
I'm just trying to make sense of the world, and the powers that damn
The powers that can, the powers that do, and do be
But these are powers of darkness that hold no power on me
For greater is He that is in me, than he thats in the world
For in me is the Christ, and it's He that the word
It is He that is the way, that is the truth, that is the life
Incomprehensible to darkness
For it is He that is the light
The One to cast upon my cares
The love that casts out all my fears
The One that it faithful, and is true
The One to wipes away all tears

The One to soon return
The One this world cannot discern
The King I long to see
My salvation that I yearn
The kingdom that's to come
My Father that I love
I'll keep my oil-lamp lit
For my righteous King above.

Truth

Truth is an ancient bolder
Embedded amid an ever-changing river of lies
Unmovable, unchanging, an eternal constant
Truth remains silent, without accusation
And those who cling to it for refuge
Must endure the rushing torrents of slanderous falsehoods
Until they too are sculpted smooth free of jagged edge
Refined In the likeness of that monument of certainty
Only then will the sun shine, and the waters abate.

Greatness is not a quality every man is imbued with.
Rather it is a distinction developed through the overcoming of adversity
That builds toward greater things to come.

Androgynous

Is that a fean or a boure
Shaam, I'm not sure
Nowadays it's not easy to tell.
Are they chatts or just fat?
A pair of stones or a gad?
Cologne or perfume, what's the smell?

Is she butch, or is he bitch?
Is this some sort switch?
Distinguishing can sometimes be tricky.
When a man's testosterone is stalled, matching a bra with his draws
Does that mean the women grow mickeys?

If hormones in the arm, could grow an inch with no harm,
And not leave you hung like an elf
For the craic it be fun, when intending the pun
Sure, who knows, you might try some yourself.

But all this confusion of unnatural illusion,
Inherently, I just cannot condone
Though the crowd shout and scream,
Leave it be, "liberty"
Yet it's a life, they wouldn't want for their own.
For grandkids are cute, with cuddles and hugs
Memories to cherish, of nurture and love
Watch them grow and bestow, your blood and your name
To disregard such a blessing, brings hypocrites shame.

Exchequer

Money for solicitors
Money for the judge.
Money for the barrister
Money for the clerk.

Money for the prisons
Money for the guards.
Money from the dealers
Suppling patsies behind bars.

Money for the defence
Money for the bar
Money for the remedy
More money for the lads.

Money for sojourners, be sure their fed and found
But no money for the native, who sleeps upon the ground.

Money for expenses
Money for their lunch
Circular economy, money for the club.

Money for the Ministers, for pensions when their done
Money for tribunals, to find where all the moneys gone?

Justice

?

?

?

Fields

Green fields all around me
A vista of verdant sea
Waves of grasslands gemstones
Uncut between the trees
Expansive precious pastures
A patchwork of allure
Emerald valleys, glens of jade
Horizons clasped, within azure.
Engraved arching furrows
That glisten with their yield
Seems like God had combed His fingers
Ploughing meadows with such ease.
Such an heirloom to be treasured
A nations family jewels
Unattainable luxuriance
Hoarded by the cruel.

Ivory Tower

Ivory tower
Full of friends
Ivory tower
They will defend

Plebs toil daily to adorn
Much to aristocratic scorn
Conceited sneers distain their sweat
As the ivory tower plots what's next

When bellies growl
And people roar
And tempers flare like high-street stores
The children cry
The mothers too
But the ivory tower safe for you
Midnight terrors
Days for fear
Once a distant theory
Now draws so near.

Chaos paves their ordered steps
Controlling all of life's aspects
Ivory Tower smug-lit chums
Bottoms up as riots burn

Ivory tower all is good
Until the great mill stone shatters all they knew.

Mommy

Oh, Mommy I can't wait
For the day that we do meet
To feel your gentle touch
Upon my little feet
Dependent as you cherish, and count my tiny toes
Swaddled in your bosom
As you kiss my button nose.
Mommy I am sorry if your labour may be hard
But I know the pain will be no more
Once safely in your arms.
Right now, I'm only growing
A tiny little bump
Just hearing your soft tender voice
Assures me of your love
I'm excited for shadows, to be lifted from my eyes
To gaze at my kind Mommy
Who parades me with such pride
You know I'll always need you
So sorry if I cry
Intreating you with craving calls, alluring lullabies.
Attentive to your comfort, as you hush me with your care
Absorbing every loving word, whispered warm within my ears.
Right now, we both are one, although with separate DNA
But I trust that you will raise me right and teach me of your ways
As the world searches for microbes, as life in outer space
You explore my beating heart
Please protect me while I wait.

Undercurrent

Beneath my gentle surface
An undercurrent flows
Rushing columns rage
Yet no one hears it roar.
My dangerous duality
Unsuspecting to your fears
I can take away your last breath
Or sweep away your cares.
Observe the sunrays dapple
Reflect sustaining light
But below my seamless streaming
Cold gushes take your life.
The courses that I've travelled
Have caused much anguished woes
Oblivious to my sudden snatch
To steal what once was yours.
Those who've known my power
Have felt my callous grip
Once deep within my torrents
I fail to let them slip
How many have fell victim
Nobody really knows
For I'm the ancient killer, who has harvests many souls.

Praise YAH

PRAISE YAH MOST HIGH
Creator of all
Praise YAH for the seasons
From blossom to fall
Praise YAH for the waters
For the clouds
For the rain
Praise YAH for the dew
For the herds
And the plains
Praise YAH for the sky
For the air
For the breeze
Praise YAH for the fruit
For the leaves
For the trees
Praise YAH for the sun
For the warmth
For the light
Praise YAH for the moon
For the stars
For the night
Praise YAH for the earth
For the soil
And its yield
Praise YAH for the flocks
For the herbs
And the fields

Praise YAH for the sea
For the fish
For the waves
Praise YAH for the mountains
For the valleys and the caves
Praise YAH for His comfort
For His Grace
For His Love
Praise YAH for His mercies
From His throne high above
Praise YAH for the cross
For the Lamb that was slain
That died with my punishment
Then rose from the grave.
Praise YAH for His Righteousness, which He imputed to me
In Yahshua my Saviour redeemed and set free.

Promise

Rebuke the deceit
Expose lies
Don't get with the program
Just listen to the word
For whoever has heard, can
Christ is the way
And forgiver of sin
He's the truth
And the life
And the Saviour of men
So, if you exist
Just too simply subsist
Then there's a gift
Free to live
In perpetual in bliss
For whoever is born just once
Will die two-fold
But when born twice
You die once
And die never, no more.

Judgment

When wrestling my demons
I just call the King
Who, will come to bring Satan and his children's defeat
The battle is done
The enemy overcome
The wise pick the side that has already won.
While the foolish think their wise
Blinded by the lies
Scoffing at the truth
Oblivious to cries, and torment
That's awaiting them dormant
Salvation is our only way out
The removal of doubt
The risen Christ
The Lord and the word
The arrogance of non-belief is absurd
Come away from the world
Here is wisdom
For those who've not heard
Distinguish light from the deception of blur
The rebuking of sin, while walking with Him
Is the only way we ever will live
And Him being Lord
The Holy Spirit and Word
Who always was
And always will be our God.
Amen.

Regret

Wake up humanity
A storm is brewing
Christ is coming
And there nowhere you're running
No where to go
No hide-y hole
For when possessions are no more
All you have left is your soul
Behold a white throne
For you were warned
But ignored
Broad and wide was how the multitudes roamed
There is no compromise
Tremble
Now meet you're demise
When giving life
You rejected the Light
Be gone from His sight
For the light rejects you
To outer darkness that is waiting for you.

My God

My Father
Who is like He?
Who can equal what's shaped of hands?
Holy Spirit
Who has knowledge like He?
Who can fathom what He understands?
My Saviour
Such compassion and grace
Who can measure His wisdom, in scale?
My God is righteous and Redeemer to all
To those who call on His name.

Salvation

I met a Christian
The boys say he preaching us nonsense
But for some strange reason
I've developed a conscience
Today's troubles are enough for today
The words of our Lord
I genuflect and I pray
But is he my Lord
If I don't obey what he says?
Faithfully, I wait for the day.
For I wasn't scared of death
Until I was faced with death
And only then was I saved from death
With a cry to the Lord
My fears and my sorrows absorbed
Peace and mercy
With his grace he bestowed
I'm so joyful I know
The Father, the Son and the Ghost
One God
Who ensures that I grow
And Nurtures my soul
Deep within, my core it matures
Christ is knocking
Why not open the door?

Patience

Meekness is not weakness
Its strength under control
Please YAH; give me strength to control.
To control all this ego, this temper and pride
To direct this resentment to die
To be more like you
To be faithful and true
But this old flesh, wars with all that is new
Hate's all that is love
Unless it favours, riches and lust
Please YAH; send me strength from above
Compel me to be patient, moreover with justice and peace
And surpass this disturbance to cease
This uproar to lapse
The wicked upheaval to collapse
Oh YAH, aid me to be humble
Encourage and comfort
Bring on Babylon's crumble
Condemn the accusers dissent
In sincerity I pray, hidden in Christ
You're servant, your son and your friend.

Grace

My flesh is ugly
Yet my Father still loves me
Even though, I never gave Him a reason
From the cross there was bleeding
Every drop covering sin
Prince of Peace, Redeemer of men
Who is like Him?
No man can conceive what He did
Giving sons, free salvation to live
Not crooked bureaucracy
Nor unbalanced scales weighed in courts
Could ever bestow such a hope
Providing Spirit of comfort, compassion and love
Every sinner justified by His Blood
Sanctified through His Spirit
No longer hid from His face
Oh YAH, you are the essence of grace.

Torch of Fidelity

To know thyself
It sounds like a noble pursuit
One of magnanimity, and enlightenment
But when we, in our frail human condition, engage this task honestly, with a genuine desire for truth, it is a journey that will lead us down the uninspiring path of lackluster and discouragement.
To know thyself, is to initially focus upon our strengths and abilities, that we subconsciously draw upon, bolstering our supposed dormant, but indeed constant egos, in the complacent ignorance, that all is well with our souls.
However, by delving deeper into the how's and why's of reason we soon discover, much to our disappointment, the petty motivations of our flawed character
Believing ourselves to be courageous, when we are rash, patient when we are irascible
truthful when boastful, and righteous when envious, (to name but a few) such dark trues come to light when we begin to illuminate our imperfect persons with the torch of fidelity.
But one man's torch of fidelity is another man's flame of shame that consumes the sustaining oxygen of arrogant self-assurance
Depending on who wields this light, and on how long it's heat can be endured, it can either be a tool of enormous personal refinement, or a scorching fire, turning to ash, that shallow barrier of combustible vanity
Such is the duality of the torch.

If an insult is posted on the Internet
And you're not online to see it
Does it make a sound?

Please Review

Dear reader,

If you enjoyed this poetry book, I would really appreciate if you could spread the word and leave a review on Amazon or Goodreads. Your opinion counts, and it influences buyer decisions on whether to purchase the book or not. Reviews can also open doors to new and bigger audiences for the author and helps get this book into the hands of those who most need to hear its message. Thank you.

Emmett

Should you wish to purchase an ebook version of the book, see the QR code below.

About the Author

Emmett Corbett is an Irish writer, poet, and lay litigant who has brought constitutional issues before the Supreme Court. Drawing from lived experience, his work confronts the hypocrisy, stonewalling, and absence of accountability within Irish state institutions, while capturing the spirit and struggle of working-class life.

He is also the author of *A Misunderstanding in Cork City*, a novella on the rowdy, raucous world of inner-city painter-decorators, and their day-to-day antics.

www.ingramcontent.com/pod-product-compliance
Lightning Source LLC
Chambersburg PA
CBHW060505080526
44584CB00015B/1561